- Who has a tummy ache?
- George's tummy hurts!

GEORGE

- Maybe George accidentally fell and hit his stomach?
Is that why his tummy hurts?
Yes or no?
- George, show the bruise on your tummy!

- Who has a tummy ache?
- Olivia has a tummy ache!
Maybe Olivia sat at the table for a long time!
Is that why her tummy hurts?
Yes or no?   **OLIVIA**

- Maybe Olivia wants to play with the children in the garden!

5

- Who has a tummy ache?
- Ali's tummy hurts!

ALI

- Maybe Ali ate too many different
treats for lunch today!
Is that why his tummy hurts?
Yes or no?

- Who has a tummy ache?
- Leon's tummy hurts!

LEON

- Maybe Leon's tummy does not like
too tight belt in shorts!
Or are these shorts too small for him?
Is that why his tummy hurts?
Yes or no?

- Who has a tummy ache?
- Hannah has a tummy ache!

HANNAH

- Maybe Hannah ate too much sweet!
Is that why her tummy hurts?
Yes or no?

11

- Who has a tummy ache?
- Nathan's tummy hurts!

NATHAN

- Maybe Nathan did not go to the toilet yesterday and today!
That is why his tummy hurts!
Yes or no?

- Who has a tummy ache?
- Xuyin's tummy hurts!

XUIN

- Maybe small gas bubbles from food are starting to form in Xuyin's tummy. Do you know how a tummy can show it? Yes or no?
The belly starts to rumble! These gas bubbles can even inflate the stomach a little...
In addition, these gas bubbles can cause severe pain in many parts of the baby's tummy!
Therefore, such children can sometimes even cry ... We are, of course, very sorry for them!
Maybe Xuyin has accumulated gas bubbles in his stomach. Yes or no?
... However, there is one little secret! When people release the accumulated gas bubbles (from the abdomen), the pain goes away!

- Who has a tummy hurts?
- Martin's tummy hurts!

16

- Maybe Martin has a stomach - ache because he wants to go to the toilet! Is that why his stomach hurts? Yes or no?
Give Martin some toilet paper, please!

- Who has a stomach - ache?
- Emma's tummy hurts!

EMMA

- Maybe Emma accidentally ate a stale
sandwich or other stale food!
Is that why her tummy hurts?
Yes or no?

- Who has a stomach - ache?
- Harry has a stomach - ache!

HARRY

- Maybe Harry does not want to eat lunch.
Is that why his stomach hurts?
Yes or no?

- Who has a stomach - ache?
- Ava has a stomach - ache!

- Maybe Ava is shy and worried!
Is that why her stomach hurts?
Yes or no?

- Who has a stomach - ache?
- Ben has a stomach - ache!

BEN

- Maybe Ben went to the toilet a few times today!
Is that why his tummy hurts?
Yes or no?

RODRIGO

- Maybe Rodrigo is afraid of something!
Is that why his stomach hurts?
Yes or no?

- Who has a stomach - ache?
- Sofia has a stomach - ache!

SOFIA

- Maybe Sofia is afraid of nausea!
Is that why her stomach hurts?
Yes or no?

- Who has a stomach - ache?
- Manuel has a stomach - ache!

MANUEL

- Maybe Manuel did not wash his
hands before eating!
Is that why his stomach hurts?
Yes or no?

Who has a tummy ache?
Svitlana Vorozhbytova